SAINT VALENTINE

the Kindhearted

Retold & Illustrated by
NED BUSTARD

ivp
Kids

This book is for my
kindhearted Leslie Anne,
with the happiest of memories
of how our love story
commenced in 1988 . . .
with a Valentine's Day card.
—N.B.

InterVarsity Press | P.O. Box 1400,
Downers Grove, IL 60515-1426 |
ivpress.com | email@ivpress.com

Text and Illustrations ©2024 by Ned Bustard

InterVarsity Press® is the publishing division
of InterVarsity Christian Fellowship/USA®.
For more information, visit www.intervarsity.org.

Scriptures taken from the Holy Bible, New International
Reader's Version®, NIrV® Copyright © 1995, 1996, 1998,
2014 by Biblica, Inc.™ Used by permission of Zondervan.
www.zondervan.com The "NIrV" and "New International
Reader's Version" are trademarks registered in the United
States Patent and Trademark Office by Biblica, Inc.™

ISBN 978-1-5140-0876-8 (print)
ISBN 978-1-5140-0877-5 (digital)

Printed in China

**Library of Congress
Cataloging-in-Publication Data**
A catalog record for this book is available
from the Library of Congress.

5 4 3 2 1 | 28 27 26 25 24

Roses are red, violets are blue,
sugar is sweet, and so are you.
This is the poem many share
to show how much they love and care.
Flowers and candy sent our way
ev'ry year on Valentine's Day.
But why the cards that say, "Be mine"?
That's all from dear Saint Valentine!

Young Valentine lived long ago
before Vivaldi or van Gogh.
The town of Terni was his home,
in Italy—just north of Rome.
The Roman Empire was quite mean,
much meaner than you've ever seen!
But Val—he had a kind, kind heart.
His care for all set him apart.

Roses are red, peas are in pods,
folks at that time worshiped false gods.
Laws required all to follow
Venus, Cupid, and Apollo.
The Romans lived unholy ways;
the one true God, they did not praise.
But Christians said, "We won't comply—
we'll worship Jesus . . . or we'll die!"

Saint Valentine worked day and night—
he lived and loved with all his might.
He shared the honey of God's Word
for the good of those who heard.
He served the holy wine and bread
and through his work God's love was spread.
But mostly Val served God above
by living out a life of love.

Roses are red, a pig's a hog,
Val loved his dad and loved his dog . . .
and his sisters *and* his brother,
and (of course!) he loved his mother.
He also was a true-blue friend—
the kind who loved up to the end.
There was no better friend to find
than our dear Saint Valentine.

Val loved his friends and family,
his care for them was plain to see.
Yet he also loved the hurting,
those who could be disconcerting—
like people who would faint away
without a warning, night or day.
Val prayed for God to bring them healing
from the falling and the reeling.

Roses are red, chocolates are best,
God said that marriages are bless'd.
But Rome's bad leader Claudius
believed it was quite obvious
that soldiers who found love were weak
—so hopes for weddings were quite bleak.
Yet, Christ bless'd weddings with fine wine,
so they were bless'd by Valentine.

For helping soldiers to get married
our dear friend Val, he soon was carried
off to a judge—in a great hall—
who asked if he was sorry at all.
The saint declared, "Christ said I should
stand up for what I know is good."
The judge said, "Show me Christ is true!"
So Val said, "Sure! What should I do?"

Roses are red, gardens take work,

laughing, the judge said with a smirk:

"Heal my blind girl . . . if Christ is real."

So Valentine at once did kneel.

After his prayer the girl could see!

The judge? He set his captive free!

Then Val said, "Here's what *you* should do:

go smash and dash each bad statue!"

The judge believed and he obeyed.
Statues came down—the judge, he prayed.
He gathered up his family,
and Val baptized them by the sea.
Forty people (*and that's not all!*)
responded to the Savior's call.
The love of God they did embrace
—of heaven's joy they all did taste.

Roses are red, rocks are rubble,

soon our saint was back in trouble!

His crime this time? He was preaching

all about God's holy teaching.

Val stood before old Claudius,

who asked, "Just what is all this fuss?

Why won't you just worship our gods,

instead of standing here at odds?"

Saint Valentine then boldly said,
"It's plain to me your gods are dead,
but Jesus lives and you will see
that he will have the victory!"

The emperor was curious,
but courtiers were furious.

So Val was cast back in a cell,
left in the dark, alone to dwell.

"*Roses are red,*" goes the old quote,
and in short notes our dear saint wrote:
"Love is patient," and "Love is kind."
"Love's not proud," and "Bear in mind:
over all virtues, put on love."
Then, as he prayed to God above,
he tied each note up with some twine
and signed them, "from your Valentine."

And as his time came to an end,
kindhearted Val worked hard to send
notes of love and of affection
to folks in every direction.
Valentine they soon did bury
the fourteenth of February.
That day each year we now recall
the kind saint who loved one and all.

Roses are red, violets are blue,

we know the love of Christ is true.

Valentine's life was filled with love—

he taught us that our God above

is the one who loves us best.

In God's great love we find our rest,

and by God's grace we can impart

his love to all . . . with all our heart.

A NOTE FROM THE AUTHOR

We don't have much information about the real Saint Valentine other than a collection of stories associated with his name. But all of these stories illustrate a life of kindness and love—love that goes beyond the typical images of romance celebrated on Valentine's Day.

It is believed that Saint Valentine was born around AD 226, and that he lived his life caring for the poor, healing the sick, and leading others to Jesus. One story says that after Valentine restored the sight of a judge's daughter, the judge broke all the idols around his house and was baptized along with his family and servants—over forty people! We honor Saint Valentine's legacy on February 14 because that's the day he was martyred for his faith. It is said that on the day Valentine was to be executed, he sent a note to the girl whose vision he had restored and signed it, "Your Valentine."

Throughout this book, you'll notice different colored hearts illustrating the different types of love that were first described by the ancient Greeks. The red hearts represent romantic love (*eros*), the green hearts represent natural love, such as the love a parent has for a child (*storge*), the blue hearts represent the love of close friends (*philia*), and the white hearts represent pure and unconditional love (*agape*).

As you read this book together, consider how the stories of Saint Valentine illustrate these four types of love. You might also identify places where these four loves show up in your own lives too!

It's that last kind of love—*agape*—that is used so often in the Bible because it describes the lovingkindness that God has for us: *pure* and *unconditional*. In fact, not only is this the extravagant love God has for us, but it's also the love that we can have for God, and the love we are invited to have for others.

Saint Valentine spent his life loving others because he knew that he was loved by God. On Valentine's Day and every day of the year, I hope the life of Valentine is a reminder to love one another—as friends, as families, and as followers of Jesus.

...Ned

And over all these good things put on love.
Love holds them all together perfectly as if they were one.

COLOSSIANS 3:14

NED BUSTARD

is a graphic designer, a children's book
illustrator, an author, and a printmaker.
As the creative director for Square Halo
Books, Inc., and curator of the Square
Halo Gallery, Ned has lectured at colleges,
schools, churches, and conferences.
His work is found in numerous titles
including *Saint Nicholas the Giftgiver*,
Saint Patrick the Forgiver, *The O in Hope*,
and *Every Moment Holy*.